Open Verdict

David Mobberley

Open Verdict

Author: David Mobberley

Copyright © David Mobberley (2023)

The right of David Mobberley to be identified as author of this work has been asserted by the author in accordance with section 77 and 78 of the Copyright, Designs and Patents Act 1988.

First Published in 2023

ISBN 978-1-915996-73-2 (Paperback)
978-1-915996-74-9 (eBook)

Cover Design and Book Layout by:
White Magic Studios
www.whitemagicstudios.co.uk

Published by:
Maple Publishers
Fairbourne Drive, Atterbury,
Milton Keynes,
MK10 9RG, UK
www.maplepublishers.com

A CIP catalogue record for this title is available from the British Library.

All rights reserved. No part of this book may be reproduced or translated by any form or by any means, electronic or mechanical, including photocopying, recording or by any information storage and retrieval system without written permission from the author.

The views expressed in this work are solely those of the author and do not necessarily reflect the views of the publisher, and the publisher hereby disclaims any responsibility for them.

By the Same Author

Equilibrium of Forces

Beneath the Darkness a Light is Shining

Sacred Journey

Revelations

First and Last

For Dwyer, Maureen, Cheryl, Miriam and Leah

'The Power of Accurate Observation is Commonly Called Cynicism by Those Who Have Not Got It'

George Bernard Shaw

CONTENTS

Cul-De-Sacs	18
The Four Seasons	18
Once Upon a Time	19
Utopian Dream	19
Doomsday	20
Beyond our Control	20
Best of Both Worlds	21
Deadly Constellation	21
Give Generously	21
Glorious	22
False Impression	22
Love in Abundance (For Philip 1964-2018)	23
High Street	23
Big brother	24
Do or Die	24
High Noon	25
Snapshot (For Jim)	25
As Nature Intended	26
Topsy - Turvy (For Joe)	26
Know Your Place (May 2018)	27
Inflation	27
Scape Goat	28
Sniper	28
Pay Back	28
Iron Curtain	29
Bullies	29
Last Hurrah	30
Nagging Doubt	30
Hidden Agenda	31
Shameful Legacy	31
Town And Country (1964-2005)	32
Little Monster (Joseph, Aged 4)	33
Damselfly	33
Meltdown	34

Battleground 34
Tightrope 34
Out of Order 35
Friend For Life 35
Earthshattering 35
Parasite – Me 36
Spooky Lucy 36
Waiting Room 37
State Of the Nation (UK 2018) 37
Boyhood Memories (Suburbs of Birmingham) 38
Never Too Late 39
Recycling 39
Prayer 40
Follow the leader 40
Freak Of Nature 41
Brief Encounter 41
USS Kentucky 42
Treasure Trove 42
Voice Mail 42
Don't Panic 43
Equilibrium Of Forces 43
Ghost 44
In His Image 44
Summer Delight 45
Double Standards 45
Young At Heart 46
Reverse Psychology 46
Post-mortem 47
Flash The Ferret (Sadly Departed) 47
Star Crazy 48
Sons Of God 48
Blue Roan (1963-79) 49
Open Verdict 49
Bright image Of a Mother Fading 50

Cats – Eyes	50
Future Past	50
Life – Cycle	51
Beauty And the Beast	51
Love	51
All In the Mind	52
Armageddon	52
Death Camp (For David Olere 1902 – 85)	53
The Tally – Ho – Club	53
Sins Of the Flesh	54
Frozen In Time	54
The Great Divide (United Kingdom)	55
The Cost of Living	55
Pure Zen	56
Psychobabble	56
The Monster Within	57
Cacophony	57
Conundrum	58
Quiet Life	58
Possessed	59
Unpredictable	59
Hellraiser	60
Life Sentence	60
Bite The Bullet (WWI)	61
All Together Now (Mantra)	61
Cars	62
White – Knuckle Climb	62
Madhouse	63
Love and Hate	63
Diabolical Regime (A Game of Salvation)	64
Jekyll And Hyde	64
Not For Sale	65
Unexpected Kill	65
Monkey Business	65

Thine Will Be Done	66
Fantasy Island	66
Game Changer	67
Dark Victory	68
Contentment	69
Great Britton	69
Blood Relatives	70
End of The Line	70
Sacrificial Lambs	71
A Bridge Too Far	71
War Crimes (Nuremberg 1946)	72
Bring Back Mr Plod	72
Halloween	73
Betwixt And Between	73
Top Secret	74
Sworn to Secrecy	74
Seeds of Destruction	75
Unfit for Office	76
Video Life	76
Hidden Secrets	76
Christmas Spirit	77
Reaper	77
The Coming of Mr X	78
Temptation	78
Pagan	79
Human Nature	79
No – Man's Land	80
Orders From Above	80
Legal Conspiracy	81
The Ultimate Warrior	81
Broken Image	82
Sacred Journey	83
Clairvoyant	84
Guiding Light	84

21st Century Apocalypse (RIP) 85
Cutting Corners 85
Rocket man 86
The Age of Plastic 86
Before And After 86
Evening Song 87
Cheryl 87
Beginning of The End (Fact or Fiction Rap) 88
Qualities of Leadership 89
Difference of Opinion 89
Food Chain 90
Horsepower 90
Empty Promises 91
Forbidden Planet 91
Living Nightmare 92
Multiple – Choice 92
Omniscient 93
Poisonous 93
Hope and Despair 94
Cheek to Cheek 94
Mindset 94
Satisfied Customer 95
Taking the Lead 95
Indigenous People 96
Yorkie 96
Berserker 97
The Last Straw 97
Manifested 98
The Departed 98
Nightmare on Vermin Street (For George) 99
Bad Chemistry 99
Rebirth 100
Joseph Stalin (1878 – 1953) 100
From the Ashes 101

Defying Gravity	101
Quantum	101
Moving On	102
Crossroad	102
Opposing Forces	102
Defect	103
Natural Selection	103
All About Eve	103
Something for Nothing	104
Blueprint	104
New President (US 2020)	105
Human Condition	105
Religious Banter	106
Recipe of Life	106
Living on The Edge (2020)	107
False Economy	107
Plasterboard Heaven	108
Aftertaste	108
Crisis Point	109
Channel Vision	109
Rosebud (For K)	110
Universal Shade	110
Breaking Point	111
Pen Pusher	111
Tough at The Top	111
Ruling Mentality	112
No Frills	112
Calculated	112
Breaking Free	113
In short Supply	113
The Heart	113
Lord of Illusion (Allegory of Creation)	114
Missed Opportunity	115
Duet	115

Falling Leaves 116
Appeasement 116
Simplicity 116
Vicious Circle 117
God 117
Modern Living 118
False Impression 118
Outrageous 118
If You Believe 119
Inverted 119
Criteria 119
Deception 120
Free – For – All 120
Hit – And – Run (October 1953) 121
Silo 121
Gods and Monsters 122
Africa 122
Deity 122
Zero 123
Castaway 123
Motorway Madness 123
Homeless 124
Severed 124
Nature Watch 124
Alarm Bells 125
Cross – Section 125
Roadmap 126
Victim of War 126
Neighbour From Hell 127
Desktop 127
The Promise 128
Spider 128
Insight 128
Heated Exchange 129

Hot Air	129
Big Solutions	129
Survivalist	130
Pulse	130
Break the Mould	130
Corrosion	131
Into the Red	131
2021	131
An Alien Called Human	132
Statement	132
Hard to Swallow	133
Out of Step	133
Aqua Man	134
Fixated	134
Ever-present	135
Fate	135
Mirror Image	135
Changing Seasons	136
Fund – Raiser	136
Mood Swings	136
Time	137
James Webb Telescope	137
Transition	138
Hill Top Hospital (Bromsgrove 1959)	138
Savile gate	138
Kayla	139
Matriarch	140
Murmuration	141
No Going Back	141
Blue Heaven	141
In The Balance	142
Worlds Apart	142
Communion	143
Rise And Fall	144

Future	144
Ancient And Modern	144
Red Tape	145
The Power of Love	145
Serial Killer	146
Rush Hour	146
Evolution Gone Mad	147
Second Coming	147
Easy Meat	148
Spontaneous Decision	148
Endless Night	149
Polaroid	149
Unity	150
Interplanetary	150
Factors	151
Loophole	151
History In the Making	151
Overgrown	152
Foretold	152
Tolerance	152
Next Generation	153
Out Of Control	153
Kid's Stuff	154
Forecast	154
Leader	155
The Unexpected	155
High Stakes (2022)	156
Crunch Time	157
Sacred Earth	157
Invasion (Ukraine 2022)	158
A New Direction	158
Dawn Chorus	159
Middle Ground	159
Problem Solved	160

Protector	160
Endgame	161
Age Of Consent	161
Potential	162
Pitfalls	162
Our Closet Neighbour	162
Afterlife	163
The Impossible Dream	163
Start To Finish	164
Genius	164
Prophecy	165
Incompatible	165
Bricklayer	166
Wisdom In Action	166
Russian Roulette	166
Out – Of – Body	167
Hybrid	167
Tartan	167
The Rape of South Wales	168
Pecking Order	168
Angels And Demons	169
Rest In Peace	169
Busy Little Bee	169
Impact	170
For God's Sake (The Bottom Line)	170
Fire and Ice	171
Rush Hour	171
Mind – Blowing	172
Rat Poison	172
Cybercops	172
Constituent Parts	173
Genesis	174
Eye Of the Beholder	174
Crash Course	175

Medium (The Art of Scrying)	175
Endeavour	176
Freedom	176
Stalker	177
Eternity	177
Extermination	178
Omen	179
A Moment in Time	179
I, Parasite	180
Out Of Sight	180
At Dawn (WW1)	181
Red Tape	181
Unfair	182
Untarnished	182
Monitored	183
Single – Minded	183
Ourselves To Blame	184
Flashbacks	184
Stalwarts	185
Straight And Narrow	185
Fireworks	185
Unpredictable	186
Second Chance	186
Imagination	187
Leap Of Faith	187
Iron Curtain 2	188
Diplomacy	188
For Better or Worse	188
Beautiful Curse	189
Revolution	189
Spread Your Wings	190
Soundscape	191
Conflict	191

Humanoid	192
Law – Abiding	192
Elizabeth R (1926 – 2022)	193
Royalty	193
Once And for All	194
Obsession (War Against Ukraine 2022)	194
Life After Death	195
One Step Behind	195
Knife – Edge (2022)	196
Enough Is Enough	196
Uncharted	197
Pied Piper	197
10/10/53	198
Seer	198
Embolism	198
Split Decision	199
Elixir of Life	199
Clinical	200
Tradition	200
Independence Day	201
Age Concern	201
Knowledge	202
Heaven and Hell	202
Bruise	202
Journey	203
Side Effects	203
Mechanics	204
Trust	204
Forever Young	205
The Unknown	205
Ecocide	206
Sitting Target	206
Race Related	206
Conviction	207

Eye For an Eye	207
Sugar and Spice	208
Brought To Book	208
Food For Thought	209
National Heroes Society	209
In a Nutshell	210
Hypocrisy	210
Bridge	210
First Contact	211
Top of the Bill (For Steven Billing, 31.1.2023)	211
Break Out	212
Antidote	212
Ordeal	212
Therapy	213
Survivor	213
Palm Sunday	213
Sacrifice	214
Defiance	214
Faith Rewarded	214
Out of control	215
Unrestrained	215
Attitude	215
Eternal	216
Milestone	216
Private Retreat	217
Hereafter	217
People Power	217
DemiGod	218
On Balance	218
Black Hole	218
Quick Fix	219
Short- Sighted	219
Closure	220

Cul-De-Sacs

Family life
Is the ultimate
Test; with its
Twists and turns
And cul-de-sac.

The Four Seasons

In the depth of winter
Are the buds of spring,
And as the bluebells
Bloom the blackbird
Sings, and with the summer
Breeze, the scent of roses
Until the acorns fall with
The autumn leaves; and then
Full circle the frost
Returns, and the snowdrops
Grow, and the robin sings.

Once Upon a Time

Imagine a world without

television, newspapers or

Mobile phones; but instead a

Village with wooden huts,

No cars or money, not a care

In the world; just living

The dream, through song

And dance, and fornication.

Utopian Dream

A classless

Society, living

In peace, without

Borders, racism

Or slavery.

Doomsday

When push comes

To shove, the rich

will take to the

Hills, and the rest

Will face oblivion.

Beyond our Control

What is the

Meaning of life?

Does anyone

Know the answer?

We can only

Hope for the best

And hide our

Apprehension.

Best of Both Worlds

Born into royalty,
But wants to be ordinary,
A foot in both camps
And a split personality.

Deadly Constellation

China is the
Rising star,
A scorpion
With a North
Korean tail.

Give Generously

At the billionaire's
Christmas party, they
Pulled crackers containing
Rolex watches, diamond
Rings, and gift aid
Envelopes for charities.

Glorious

Magnificent, majestic,

Gothic perfection; heaven

On earth is Lincoln Cathedral.

False Impression

He went down to

His local market,

And Purchased a

Rolex watch, he

went to the pub,

But was later

Found mugged and

The twenty quid

Fake was missing.

Love in Abundance
(For Philip 1964-2018)

He died in his

Sleep, aged 54;

A difficult life

From start to finish;

But on the day

of his funeral,

A total surprise,

A church full

of people to say

Their goodbyes.

High Street

For saving lives, a

Defibrillator on the outside wall

Of a funeral parlour.

Big brother

He really is a

know-all, a finger

In every pie, all

Our details are

Inside his head,

And he pretends

To be democratic.

Do or Die

When the end

Gets closer, I

Will move to

The past, and

Hope to return

In the future.

High Noon

The threat
Of war is
Back in town;
Trigger – happy,
Head-to-head,
Quickest
On the draw.

Snapshot
(For Jim)

A friend,
A teacher,
An atheist
At heart;
And he left
His body
To science.

As Nature Intended

Growing old gracefully

Takes years of practice, only

For the young at heart.

Topsy - Turvy
(For Joe)

You mustn't do this,

And you shouldn't do

That, is you eat too

Much you're going

To get fat, but he

still has a drink,

The occasional cigar,

He eats what he likes

In his ninety fifth year.

Know Your Place
(May 2018)

On the same day as
The 2018 cup final,
A royal wedding took
Place at Windsor Castle;
Inside the grounds the
Royals and celebrities,
Paraded past cameras
On their way to the chapel;
But outside the walls,
Behind metal barriers,
The general public
Waved their flags.

Inflation

In the past we talked
In millions today it's
All about the billions,
Tomorrow it will turn
Into trillions, but what
About the zillions? -
I've lost interest!

Scape Goat

Looking for someone
To blame; anybody
Will do, as long as
It's not me or you.

Sniper

Detached, yet connected,
Dispassionate, yet committed,
Caught in the cross hairs,
Despatched from a distance.

Pay Back

Poachers went hunting
For rhinos but were eaten by
A pack of lions.

Iron Curtain

Life and death
Walk side by side,
Paper thin but
A great divide.

Bullies

Bullying starts
At home! It moves
Into schools, and
Places of work,
And it drives
Along the road.

Last Hurrah

If I get the
Chance, before
The bombs go.
Off, I will have
A cigar, a glass
Of wine, and
Make love to a
Beautiful woman.

Nagging Doubt

Sometimes, when
Sitting alone, I
Wonder if I'm
Human or is there
Something else
Inside, like an
Angel or a demon.

Hidden Agenda

A perfect world,

Filled with perfect

People, was never

God's intention.

Shameful Legacy

Through wars and

Poverty, millions

Of children have

Needlessly died.

Never given the

Chance to prove

Their true potential.

Town And Country
(1964-2005)

I left school with

Minimal qualifications,

But secured a job at a

City centre chemist – old –

Established – manufacturing

Medicines: I stayed six

Years and loved every

Minute, but when they

Left that building, I

Moved to the country, and

Worked as a postman

Until I retired.

Little Monster
(Joseph, Aged 4)

Under three feet

Tall, with a mischievous

Face, out of control

And full of cheek

The devil incarnates,

He belongs in a box,

And only let out when

Grandma comes round.

Damselfly

She crawled out

Of the river, and

Changed overnight.

An emerald princess

With gossamer wings.

Meltdown

As the world's economy
Crashes, Nuclear war approaches,
Annihilation beckons.

Battleground

A malevolent universe,
Forever unfolding, Almighty God
And his bitter rival.

Tightrope

As we walk
The knife – edge
Of existence
We must keep.
Our balance or
Face extinction.

Out of Order

Take away the discipline

And it all falls down.

Anarchy, revolution are

The new kids in town.

Friend For Life

If hope is

Waiting to say

'Hello' shake

His hand and

Don't let go.

Earthshattering

Global warming:

An ice age coming.

Tectonic plates shifting,

An asteroid crashing,

The sun exploding.

Parasite – Me

From pillar to post

On the back of others.

Wrapped up and protected

From a hostile world.

Spooky Lucy

She appears when I

Least expect it, the

Lady I once knew at

Work: I can see her

Face, and hear her

Voice, but I know

She died last year.

Waiting Room

Going to the doctor's
Is a painful experience.
Where the side effects
Outweigh the treatment.

State Of the Nation
(UK 2018)

Politics, politics, what
A load of bollatics; a
Government in crisis,
And lead by a bunch
Of headless chickens.

Boyhood Memories
(Suburbs of Birmingham)

I moved to Sparkhill

In 1956; and lived in

A house on the Stratford

Road: it was on a main

Bus route by the 'mermaid'

Pub, with the Piccadilly

Cinema next door. I joined

The Cubs, and sang in a

Choir, played in the grounds

Of the 'Conservative' Club I

Attended St John's, the junior

School, where I fell in love

With Jennifer King, but

She went to Australia, before

I moved to Kings Heath.

Never Too Late

To succeed in life

Is to realise your dreams, before you

Become part of history.

Recycling

We buy, we sell,

We produce the waste.

We dump, we burn,

We recycle the rest.

We live, we die, we

Get rid of remains,

But some believe

We come back again.

Prayer

When I talk to God, I
Know he's listening, and
I feel his presence as
He gives his blessing, and
The strength to carry on.

Follow the leader

In a sheep
Driven world,
Be careful who
You follow, then
Go with the
Flow, or become
An outsider.

Freak Of Nature

Human beings are

Complex creatures.

Neither good nor bad

But easily swayed.

With the capacity

To learn education

Is essential, but

Being human makes

Us unpredictable.

Brief Encounter

A glance in reception,

A drink at the bar,

Sex in the evening,

After breakfast, they

Leave in their cars.

USS Kentucky

Nuclear powered.

Undetectable; with

The firepower to

Destroy a country.

Treasure Trove

My hero is Sir Walter

Raleigh: he brought back potatoes,

Tobacco and coffee.

Voice Mail

Suddenly, a message

From spirit, delivered

By Phill Harben, a

TV chef from the 1950s.

Don't Panic

Radio signals from

Outer space; aliens

Are coming, a flash

Of light; they're here!

Equilibrium Of Forces

Black and white,

Good and bad,

Life and death,

Happy and sad.

Science and religion,

Hot and cold,

Yin and yang

Young and old.

Ghost

In the dead
Of night, he
Walks about,
Moaning and
Groaning, and
Carrying his head.

In His Image

Out of timeless
Space came a
Digital God; he
Pressed his keyboard
And created light.
He multiplied, divided,
Added and subtracted,
Until evolution
Produced mankind.

Summer Delight

In sun-drenched meadows,

The constant drone of honeybees

Collecting nectar.

Double Standards

Politicians

Pretend to

Care; but it's

Not about

Us, it's all

About them.

Young At Heart

Pulling faces,

Making noises,

Acting silly,

Running wild.

Grandad thinks

He's in the

Playground acting

Like a child.

Reverse Psychology

As you get older,

Time becomes quicker,

But if you want to

Live longer, forget

About time, and try

To think younger.

Post-mortem

On the day of his
Funeral, a morning
Cremation, with hymns
And music, and the
Vicar's address; but
After the service he
Left with two strangers,
One was an angel, and
The other a demon!

Flash The Ferret
(Sadly Departed)

White as snow; quick as
Lighting; playful and naughty,
Nose into everything.

Star Crazy

The world messiah

Means sacred being.

Not footballer, Rockstar

Or political leader.

Sons Of God

Nuclear

Physicists

Saw the

Light; the

Big Bang

Theory inside

A bomb.

Blue Roan
(1963-79)

A dog in a million

Was beautiful Bruno.

Now a magical beast

In the world of spirit.

Open Verdict

Once, while looking

Into a bevel – edged.

Mirror, strong sunlight

From a window opposite,

Struck the glass, and

Framed my image with

Spectral colours; moved

By the experience, I

Questioned the laws of

Physics in the light

Of a mystical evidence.

Bright image Of a Mother Fading

Once, a force ten

Wind, is now a gentle

Breeze, moving slowly

Towards a higher plane.

Cats – Eyes

After dark on country roads,

Small black cats, who sleep by day,

Wake up, and in single file along

The middle, lead the blind to safety.

Future Past

The future becomes the

Past before the present

Has time to settle.

Life – Cycle

We come on the morning tide,

And stay through the afternoon,

The setting sun brings forth humility,

By midnight our footsteps have gone.

Beauty And the Beast

In a beautiful world

The colour of money

Has turned people ugly.

Love

The power of love

Is blind to class

And beyond the

Reach of money.

All In the Mind

One day,

The mind

Will engulf

The body,

And thought

Will absorb

The spirit.

Armageddon

When man met God and Satan,

In a show- down at sunrise,

All hell broke loose, and heaven responded.

And while the serpent raped the virgin eve,

The butchered Christ wept tears of blood.

The armies of two heavens clashed,

The tree of life was the victor's prize.

And when the conflict ended,

And the nuclear age defused

A hybrid child came from the womb,

And suppressed his hate with love.

Death Camp

(For David Olere 1902 – 85)

Young artist

In Auschwitz.

Survived the

War; dark images

Of inhumanity.

The Tally – Ho – Club

Resplendent huntsmen on

Horseback, chasing a fox

To ground, allowing their

Hounds to tear it apart, and

They call it vermin control.

Sins Of the Flesh

Lust and passion
Are hard to control,
When desire becomes
Unbearable, but
For all concerned,
Forbidden fruit is.
Morally unacceptable.

Frozen In Time

While sitting in the
Local churchyard, I
Noticed a grave set
Apart from the rest.
It had two rag dolls, one
Standing on either side
Of a black marble book.
And on the left – hand
Page, the inscription
Read, 'In Loving Memory
Of Michelle Louise,
Born Asleep 1975'.

The Great Divide
(United Kingdom)

In a country still

Marred by division –

North and South,

Ethnic minorities, the

Old boy network, with

Total injustice swept

Under the carpet; the

Anguish of poverty, the

Grandeur of wealth,

With no chance of

Changing the system.

The Cost of Living

A life full

Of action,

Consequences

And pay back.

Pure Zen

In the eye of a

Storm is a peaceful place, where

God and nature coexist.

Psychobabble

The psychic

Psychologist

Went to see his

Psychiatrist

And asked for

Psychanalysis,

Which ruled out

Psychosis, but revealed

Paranormal

Activity.

The Monster Within

Beyond the unconscious is

Our primitive self; our basic instincts,

Controlled by the id.

Cacophony

Mobile phones ringing,

Exhaust pipes blowing,

Plastic bottles clunking,

Car doors banging,

Computer keyboards clicking,

Loud music blasting,

Human brains exploding.

The noise is never-ending.

Conundrum

Is it best

To think

First, or

Act before

Thinking?

Quiet Life

Teenagers are

Out of control,

Because adults

Say 'Yes' when

They really mean

'No'. Bring back

National Service!

Possessed

Human beings like

To own things; like

Objects, animals and

Each other; some

People call it love,

But for others it

Becomes an obsession.

Unpredictable

The weather

Has a mind of

Its own; and a

Temper to match.

Hellraiser

While surfing the
Dark Web, I met a
Demon, who showed
Me angels fighting
In a blood drenched
Heaven; and the human
Race impaled on stakes,
With the constant sound
Of breaking glass,
As the chimes rang
Out at midnight.

Life Sentence

Is being told you
Are terminally ill,
With only a short time
To live, any different
From being sentenced
To death, for a crime
You didn't commit.

Bite The Bullet
(WWI)

Over the top, the tommies went,
Under a hail of bullets, but
Some survived to tell the tale,
Of indiscriminate carnage.

All Together Now
(Mantra)

We are all alive
For a reason, all
Part of the human
Race, some people
We like, and others
We hate, but life
Is for living –
GET ON WITH IT!

Cars

A brilliant

Invention for

Getting about.

But speeding,

Aggression and

CO2, is the

Price, we pay

For convenience.

White – Knuckle Climb

When climbing

Mountains in

Patagonia, take

A set of paddles,

In case of a

Rapid decent.

Madhouse

Everything
Has gone to
The dogs; the
World is
Barking mad.

Love and Hate

Best friends
Today,
Sworn enemies
Tomorrow.

Diabolical Regime
(A Game of Salvation)

Was God being

Serious when he

Created mankind,

Or are the devil

And he really partners,

With a wicked

Sense of humour.

Jekyll And Hyde

In less than an hour,

The sea can turn from

A ten- headed hydra with

Attitude, into a pussy cat

Without any teeth.

Not For Sale

A working farm

In the middle

Of London, used

To educate people.

Unexpected Kill

The ferret went

Down a rabbit

Hole, but found a

Poisonous snake.

Monkey Business

Because Darwin

Said we came from

Apes, Adam changed

Into Tarzan, and Eve

Became Jane, and

Fed him bananas.

Thine Will Be Done

The bible tells

Us to love thy

Neighbour, and

I sometimes do,

If she's willing.

Fantasy Island

In a perfect world,

The sky is blue, the

Grass is green, and

Everybody loves each

Other; one big happy

Family, living and

Working in perfect

Harmony, and never

A cross word spoken.

Game Changer

Education can

Change perception,

And rid the world

Of ignorance.

Dark Victory

Immortal,
Belligerent,
Cast out
Of heaven.
Driven by hate
And retribution.
Devious,
Cunning,
Misunderstood.
Harbinger
Of chaos.
Collector
Of souls.
With lies and
Deception,
Mankind is
Defeated; the
War of attrition
Is won; the
Gates of heaven
Are closed forever.
The wrath of
Satan begun.

Contentment

They say the

Grass is greener

On the other side,

But I prefer

The beach, and

The incoming tide.

Great Britton

A constable masterpiece

Of pastoral beauty, and framed by

A golden coastline.

Blood Relatives

Modern cavemen live

In houses, they go down

The pub, and to football

Matches: they wear nice

Clothes, and drive fast

Cars, they use computers,

And make love slowly.

But deep down inside,

They remain primeval.

End of The Line

Royalty is part of our

Heritage; and the Queen

Has done her duty; but after

Her death, we must call

It a day, and install

An elected republic.

Sacrificial Lambs

Serial killers get

Celebratory status.

Television, newspapers,

Books and films; but

Who remembers their

Victims, unless they're

Jack The Ripper's.

A Bridge Too Far

Humpback bridges are

For cars and horses,

Not thirty-ton trucks

Taking shortcuts.

War Crimes
(Nuremberg 1946)

They honestly believed what they

did was right; showed no remorse when

Confronted with the truth.

Bring Back Mr Plod

The old – fashioned bobby

Used to walk his beat.

He knew all the people,

And helped where he could.

But the modern police

Force is all about cuts,

And front-line coppers

In high – speed cars.

Halloween

November eve – the
Samhain festival, with
Witches, pumpkins and scary
Masks, trick – or – treat, and
Bonfires burning, Michael
Myers is back in town!

Betwixt And Between

Sex is great when
You're single, in
Marriage it can lose
Its spark, divide the
Two, and true love
Wins, but passion
Requires a lover.

Top Secret

Lots of clever people,

Using technology to

Improve the world; but

A few clever people,

In secure locations, are

Producing lethal weapons.

Sworn to Secrecy

If you want

To find out

What goes on

In high places,

Ask the cleaner,

The chauffeur,

The civil servant.

Seeds of Destruction

I make the transition

From equation to bomb.

I broke the will of a nation,

And ended the war.

I produce plutonium

And toxic waste.

I'm hard to control

And difficult to store.

I find ways to escape,

And contaminate land,

I will enter the food chain

And damage your genes,

I will live forever

And watch you die,

I will rule the world

When you become extinct.

I am the legacy

Of a nuclear age,

And I thrive on radiation.

Unfit for Office

Rich politicians are a

Thorn in the side; an anathema

To ordinary people.

Video Life

Switched on at birth; go

Fast – forward; can't rewind; at

The end rejected.

Hidden Secrets

Family secrets come

Out to play – abortion,

Adoption, adultery,

Incest. Nobody's perfect!

Christmas Spirit

Singing carols, and

Buying presents,

Having dinner, and

Family arguments.

Reaper

Death is a ghost

That haunts mankind.

It enters the body,

And releases the sole.

The Coming of Mr X

Tall, dark and handsome.

Blonde, short and weak,

Academically brilliant,

At home with a shovel and

Pick; a ladies' man, with

A feminine voice, can drive

A Porsche, or a Chieftain tank.

Built like an athlete but

Hopeless at sport, a wonderful

Son to his motherless father.

On a crowded street he appears

Mr average, but beneath

His hair an indelible

Number – hell and damnation,

His gift to mankind.

Temptation

Christ in the wilderness,

Tired and hungry – offered the

World on a plate.

Pagan

From the acorn

Grows the mighty

Oak; beneath its

Boughs the

Druid speaks.

Human Nature

Like a hot

Volcano –

Violent

Unpredictable

Self – destructive.

No – Man's Land

Between heaven and
Hell is a nightmare
World, where good
And evil fight for
Supremacy, and share
The spoils of war.

Orders From Above

In wartime you must
Kill the enemy, in
Peacetime it becomes a
Crime, the bible tells us
'Thou Shall Not Kill', and
Never question authority.

Legal Conspiracy

Loopholes in

The law, begin

With government,

Used by barristers,

Endorsed by judges.

The Ultimate Warrior

On the battlefield

Of life we must stand

Our ground, in the fight

To conquer evil; and

With the weapons of love

And peace, we can win

The war, and enter

The gates of heaven.

Broken Image

At the heart of creation is
The mind of God; a complex
Being, with an alter – ego, a
Double – edged sword, quenched
In the blood of angels; he
Divided Heaven and created
Hell. A loving God, who devised
Mankind, but invented death.
A merciful God, with a violent
Temper, who tempted eve to
Commit a sin. His true identity
Remains a mystery; but God almighty
Is both good and evil! And in
This state of eternal conflict,
Humankind must seek salvation.

Sacred Journey

Fate is the road

That begins at birth.

The route is straight

And lined with fences.

The human race in

Single file must

Climb the hills and

Cross the bridges.

Until we reach the

Point of death, where

The body dies, but

The soul is saved.

Its destination

Is preordained.

Clairvoyant

In a crystal ball

She saw his future,

And said a stranger

Would change his life.

Dressed in white, with

A crown of thorns and

His name is Jesus Christ.

Guiding Light

God is the master

  Who crafted my fate.

    He opened my eyes

      To the beauty within.

        With the power of faith

          I will overcome death.

            And enter the realms

              Of eternal peace.

21st Century Apocalypse
(RIP)

As we entered the 21st century,

The devil came, with his bag of tricks.

Values and morals went out

Of the window; animal behaviour

Became the norm; self – preservation,

And fuck you Jack, in a meltdown world

Filled with fucked up government; and

When the finger of destiny pushed,

The earth imploded and disappeared.

Cutting Corners

The world of

Convenience

Is destroying

The planet.

Rocket man

Behind the president

Is the man in black.

Inside his case, are

The launching codes

To Armageddon.

The Age of Plastic

Wonderful,

Marvellous,

Great invention.

Poisonous, toxic,

Endless pollution.

Before And After

When two brothers,

Discovered they'd

Been adopted, they

Still had nothing in

Common, but remained

Adopted brothers.

Evening Song

Between Lincoln Castle and the
Cathedral, is a public square,
Where a blackbird sings his song,
In a tree by the Roman ruins.

Cheryl

Both divorced, but
Remain unmarried.
We live in a flat, where
We share finances; she
Is my rock, the love of
My life, the nuts and
Bolts, my guiding light.

Beginning of The End
(Fact or Fiction Rap)

In the beginning, a huge explosion,
The universe expanding, the solar
System, the garden of Eden or evolution,
Science fact, or religious fiction?
Top of the tree, are human beings, our
Brains are crammed with big ideas,
But we abuse the planet, and drain
Resources, while nature plans her
Retribution: but here we are in the
21st century, technology mad, and
Overcrowded, nuclear weapons, or climate
Change, choose your poison and die in vain;
Or begin to pray, and seek forgiveness,
Science fact, or religious fiction?
Or begin to pray, and seek forgiveness,
Science fact, or religious fiction?

Qualities of Leadership

Strength of mind,

With a cast – iron

Will; sensitive,

Compassionate, with

The common touch.

Easy to approach,

Prepared to listen,

But ruthless when

The need arises.

Difference of Opinion

Some say yes,

But others say

No, these so –

Called experts

Who disagree.

Food Chain

In the middle
Of a wood, as a
Deer was feeding,
A hunter was
Hiding behind a
Tree, but a bear
Came up and
Killed him, and
The deer got
Away scot – free.

Horsepower

Still being used today,
Are the log – pulling ponies
Of the past; strong as
An OX, with amazing
Endurance, they transport
The timber, from the woods
To the road, where lorries
And trucks take over.

Empty Promises

Somethings never

Change, like people

Who promise to do

Their best, but end

Up doing nothing.

Forbidden Planet

Too many people,

Not enough food,

Climate change,

Shortage of water,

Civil unrest, the

World at war

Scientists fail

To find a solution.

Ethnic cleansing,

Survival of the

Fittest, world

On the brink,

No second coming.

Living Nightmare

Ebola is the
Devil's virus
Evolving, and
Searching for
Weakness; its
Teeth are large,
But its claws
Are sharper.
Vigilance
Is paramount.

Multiple – Choice

Human beings
Are male or
Female; hetero,
Bi, or homosexual.
But times have
Changed, with gender –
Neutral, and the
Freedom to
Choose which one.

Omniscient

According to the bible,

God is almighty – all – knowing,

All – seeing; but a jealous

God, vengeful and unforgiving.

But believe it or not,

When the going gets

Tough, he is the light

At the end of the tunnel.

Poisonous

Some people thrive on

Causing trouble; it is

In their nature, their

Bread and butter; beware

Of malicious intent.

Hope and Despair

Side by side,

Hand in hand, a

Thin red line,

A great divide.

Cheek to Cheek

When dancing close

Together, it's like

Having sex with

Your clothes on.

Mindset

Freedom is a

State of mind.

To act and

Speak in public,

Or to keep

It all inside.

Satisfied Customer

When looking in the
Shopwindow of life,
Don't buy what you
Cannot afford, don't envy
Others, or wait for the
Sales, but be happy
With what you've got.

Taking the Lead

Taking the dog for
A walk, is a national
Institution; the owners
Find it therapeutic,
But most dogs can
Take it or leave it.

Indigenous People

Sitting on top of Uluru, as the sun
Begins to rise, an elder plays the
Didgeridoo, as the red earth comes
A live; on the plains of North America,
Where the buffalo once roamed, the
Sound of drums, and Indians dancing,
As the shaman sings his song.

Yorkie

From the science fiction
Film 'Flight of the Navigator',
Comes the alien creature called
A Puckmaren; we recently bought
One, and called him George.

Berserker

Whether Anglo – Saxon,

Medieval, or Viking,

This warrior class

Would never give in.

Their sole objective

Was to Kill! Kill! Kill!

With a club, sword

Or two – Handed axe.

The Last Straw

When told by

The doctor he

Had six months

To live, he got

In first, and

Died of shock.

Manifested

Hollow promises

To tempt the

Voters; full

Of loopholes,

Easily flushable.

Bring back

Guy Fawkes.

The Departed

Where have all

The people gone,

The ones we

Used to know?

They are waiting

On the other side,

They are waiting

For me and you.

Nightmare on Vermin Street
(For George)

Not a Doberman, or

Rottweiler, but a

Yorkshire terrier; with

Dish like ears, Freddy

Krueger claws, and

A set of teeth like Jaws.

Bad Chemistry

Hate is a potent weapon.

Love is also destructive, but

Mix them both together, and

The outcome is catastrophic.

Rebirth

The seasons come, and
The seasons go, the oak leaves
Fall, but the acorns grow.

Joseph Stalin
(1878 – 1953)

He was born in Georgia:
From humble beginnings; and
Was part of the revolution.
Self – preservation was the name
Of the game, until he become
Their leader. He ran rings
Around his opponents, and
Helped defeat the German
Army, he led foreign leaders
Up the garden path, and changed
The face of Europe; but after 30
Years of abusing his people,
This 'man of steel', collapsed and
Died, a genius or a psychopath,
Only history will decide.

From the Ashes

After World War
Three, the cockroach
Emerged victorious.

Defying Gravity

When newton saw the
Apple fall, he didn't see
The bird in flight.

Quantum

Electrons,
Protons,
Neutrons,
Quarks.
Neutrinos,
Strings, multi –
Dimensions.

Moving On

When things

Breakdown

And fall apart,

It's time to

Leave and

Start again.

Crossroad

If you can summon

The devil, there must

Be a God, but who will

You choose to follow?

Opposing Forces

The star of Bethlehem, the

Blood red moon, the light of creation,

The harbinger of doom.

Defect

Robots with
Attitude are
Dangerous!

Natural Selection

Strong
Winds
Break the
Weakest
Branches.

All About Eve

Given free will,
She chose the
Apple, God
Passed judgement,
But the Devil
Claimed victory.

Something for Nothing

Young kids looking

After their parents,

The old taking care

Of their own, the

Government departments

Are rubbing their

Hands, at all the

Money they're saving.

Blueprint

Behold the earth

In all its glory.

Everything planned,

Nothing is random.

New President
(US 2020)

Only old

Men and

Billionaires

Need apply.

Human Condition

The four

Essentials

That make

Us tick, are

Alcohol, drugs,

Nicotine

And sex.

Religious Banter

Love and

Hate, good

And evil, God

Above, death

And Satan.

Recipe of Life

Love and

Happiness,

Suffering

And pain, with

A spoonful

Of luck for

Good measure.

Living on The Edge
(2020)

The world in crisis

Because of coronavirus.

The economic tightrope

Beginning to fray,

Everything centred around

Money and finance, but

The world on a knife –

Edge is going to bleed.

False Economy

They promise you

This, and they promise

You that, but when

It really matters, you

Get nothing back.

Plasterboard Heaven

I live in a block
Of flats, and each
Room is a hollow box,
Eleven homes on three
Levels, with 37 steps
In between. In the
Summer the heat is
Unbearable, doors closing.
On the bottom can be
Heard on the top, the
Whole building shakes
When they empty the
Bins, hooray for
Modern construction.

Aftertaste

Revenge is
Sweet but
Forgiveness
Is sweeter.

Crisis Point

Thank you, John,

And Nikita, for

Saving the world

In 62, but will

Common sense prevail

Next time, or will

The hawks win out,

And destroy us all?

Channel Vision

Don't look for

Faults where

None exist, but

Walk a straight

Line with your

Eyes wide open.

Rosebud
(For K)

Well on her way to

Becoming a woman.

A beautiful rose in

The garden of Eden

Universal Shade

Black and

White, brown

And yellow,

Mixed together

Make one colour.

Breaking Point

Constant pressure is

The weapon of choice, to change

The mind of government.

Pen Pusher

Pen and paper,

Clipboard ready,

Tick, tick, tick,

Tick – box Barbe.

Tough at The Top

Government

Ministers are

Ten – a – penny.

Here today and

Gone tomorrow

Ruling Mentality

Governments are good at stepping
Up, but then walking away and
Leaving it to charities; high – speed
Trains, and modern buildings, seem
More important than ordinary people.

No Frills

The observations
Of an ordinary
Man, are simple,
Concise, straight
To the point.

Calculated

Never got to be a
Mathematician; but
I come at life from
A different angle.

Breaking Free

Conditioned by

Others to be

Something you're

Not? Throw off

The shackles, and

Never look back.

In short Supply

Optimism is a

Potent drug; it's the

Opiate of success.

The Heart

A muscular pump,

With four chambers

And valves; numerous

Vessels and eight

Pints of blood.

Lord of Illusion
(Allegory of Creation)

Out of the blue,
The darkness divided
Like the red sea did
For Moses; and a
Figure in white led
Me down the tunnel, to
The foot of a golden
Throne; and on either
Side was Adam and Eve,
Underneath was the
Serpent Satan, but sat
In his chair was the
Invisible man, and his
Name was Imagination.

Missed Opportunity

Somewhere in
Chad, is a six
Year old boy,
Who if given
The chance could
Become a doctor.

Duet

The constant
Drone of the
Motorway; in
Tune with my
Didgeridoo.

Falling Leaves

Money doesn't grow on
Trees; but for the super – rich,
Their autumn never ends.

Appeasement

Public enquiries are looking
For answers, but bending the truth
And shifting the blame.

Simplicity

Make it
Simple.
Keep it
Simple.
Simple
Is best.

Vicious Circle

So here we are

At the 21st chapter

Of revelation; and

With the conflict

Over, a new Jerusalem,

A new world order,

With God at the centre,

But no longer invisible.

But humankind, now

Made immortal, must

Face the truth, and

Bow down to Satan.

God

At the centre on an

Endless Maze, is a door in

The middle of nowhere.

Modern Living

Housing estates are
Full of boxes; no
Front gardens, only
Off – road parking.

False Impression

Governments are supposed
To serve their people, but
End up serving themselves.

Outrageous

How wonderful it
Is to be ordinary.
To see life from
Every angle; to
Watch the richer
Get richer and the
Poorer get poorer.
In a world full of
Hate and corruption.

If You Believe

God's love is

Overwhelming.

Unconditional,

Everlasting.

Inverted

While nailed

To the cross,

He left his

Body; descended

Into hell, and

Never came back.

Criteria

Three ways to reach the

Top, good education, strong personality,

And does your face fit.

Deception

Half-truths are
Better than lies,
Unless they're
Proved untruthful.

Free – For – All

Missions
To mars
Could open
The door
To greedy
Investors.

Hit – And – Run
(October 1953)

Run over by a

Stolen car; five

Years old, and I

Should have died.

A fractured skull

Was the only scar,

From my first

Encounter with death.

Silo

Four colleagues on

Duty when the order

Came; three shot in

The head, one left

To press the button.

Gods and Monsters

Were Hitler
And Starlin part
Of god's plan,
Or did they rise
Up from the
Bowels of hell?

Africa

A beautiful animal,
Caught in a trap, its
Insides ripped out by
Greed and corruption.

Deity

I don't believe
In royalty, and yet
I believe in God.
But the Queen is just
A woman and God
Is beyond belief.

Zero

The key to
Inner peace,
Is outwardly
Doing nothing!

Castaway

If asked for my
Luxury item, on
'Desert Island
Discs' I would
Opt for a radio,
With BBC Four.

Motorway Madness

Remove the hard
Shoulder, to help
Congestion, call
It 'Smart' and wait
To get killed.

Homeless

If everything goes out
Of the window, and your
Bed is under a bridge,
Rock bottom becomes your
Postcode, and it could
Happen to you or me.

Severed

When death is ready
To take your life,
He will cut the cord,
And set you free.

Nature Watch

The English countryside
Is full of surprises, stings, and bites,
And big cats hunting.

Alarm Bells

Nature has been

Talking for years.

But mankind is

Beginning to listen.

Cross – Section

In a box

Of assorted

Colours, are

Straight,

Bisexual,

Gay and

Transgender.

Roadmap

On the palm

Of your hand,

Is the whole

Of your life,

Mapped out in a

Series of lines.

Victim of War

From refugee, to illegal

Immigrant; works in a factory,

Lives in a hovel.

Neighbour From Hell

The devil lives

At number six.

He looks okay

From a distance,

But his eyes are

Black, and he

Never sleeps,

And he likes to

Eat raw liver.

Desktop

A cigar cutter shaped

Like a guillotine, by a skull

From the French Revolution.

The Promise

On easter Sunday,
Celebration, choirs of angels, the
Resurrection, God Almighty.

Spider

Between two branches he
Spins his web, a silken trap
To catch his prey.

Insight

Suddenly, in a vision,
Intense green light; a
Blueprint of my life,
Mapped out and viewed
From above; a network
Of interconnecting lines,
Covered in strange 3D
Symbols; incomprehensible!
But a glimpse into
The mind of God.

Heated Exchange

Like pack ice in

Summer, the cold war ended

In Nuclear Winter.

Hot Air

Politicians who promise the most,

Are the ones who deliver the least.

Big Solutions

Better education,

Family planning,

Job security,

Affordable housing,

Public transport,

Cleaner energy,

Recycling waste,

Eating less meat.

Survivalist

African, poor, uneducated.

Scraping a living from landfill.

Treated like garbage.

Pulse

Head – splitting frequency,

Silently delivered, maximum damage,

The ultimate weapon.

Break the Mould

Don't do what's

Expected; go

Your own way,

Be different.

Corrosion

Greed and envy have

Turned capitalism toxic.

Into the Red

A loan is a

Loan, until it

Becomes a debt.

2021

Born on Wednesday the

1st of September; long life and

Happiness, Matalia Elizabeth.

An Alien Called Human

We arrived from outer
Space; and went across
Endless oceans; through
Tropical forests, to the polar
Regions; the perfect planet
To start again, a second
Chance to get it right.

Statement

Overlooking a motorway
Near London, a giant white angel,
Created by a Black artist.

Hard to Swallow

Sex is for

Pleasure and

Reproduction.

But too much

Sex, without

Precautions,

Means too many

People, and

Not enough

Food and water.

Out of Step

A son of the

20th century.

Finding it hard

To adapt to

Modern living; but

Helped by those

Who love him.

Aqua Man

We crawled out

Of the ocean, and

Lived on the land, but

Fundamentally we

Are made of water.

Fixated

The sun in your face,

Is a thing of the past.

Your mobile phone has

All the answers; the world

At your feet, and it

Fits in your pocket.

Ever-present

It was there before
I was born; it will be
There long after I'm
Gone; it will always be
There, the power of God,
Until the end of time.

Fate

He knew in advance
Of his crucifixion,
His betrayal by Judas,
And denial by Peter.

Mirror Image

Behind your reflection is
Another you, an alternative world, on
The opposite side of the sun.

Changing Seasons

Hardship is drought in
Summer, floods in winter, drought
In spring and autumn.

Fund – Raiser

After military action,
And natural disasters,
Charities are left to
Pick up the pieces.

Mood Swings

Love is unconditional.
Trust, we have to earn;
Hate is soul destroying,
Anger releases pressure.

Time

From ancient man,

To the present day.

Using the sun, calendars

And astrophysics.

Always in a hurry,

To get things done,

Before the end of

Our allotted span.

James Webb Telescope

It cost $10 billion

To build; 100x

More powerful than

'Hubble', successfully

Launched on Christmas

Day; its main objective

To see the beginning,

And whatever lies beyond.

Transition

He died in his sleep.
Awoke in the morning – a different
World, no longer mortal!

Hill Top Hospital
(Bromsgrove 1959)

Open – heart surgery,
Aged 11; six long weeks in a
fairy tale castle, idyllic.

Savile gate

From dance hall owner to TV
Presenter; a household name and
Prime Ministers favourite; he
Mixed with royalty, made millions
For charity, did voluntary work
In hospitals, children's homes
And mortuaries; suspected of
Perversion, but never convicted,
Until after his death in 1984.

Kayla

Not related by blood,

But she calls me grandad.

And from the time she

Was born, to the present day,

She is the apple of her

Grandad's eye; and if I

Had a choice, she would be

The daughter I never had.

Matriarch

Margret Thatcher was a

Greengrocer's daughter; she

Did well at school, and went

To university, where she got

Two degrees, one in law, the

Other in chemistry. She entered

Politics, and became Prime

Minister, preferring financial

To the manufacturing sector.

She destroyed the miners, and

Weakened the union, her biggest

Allie was Ronald Reagan; but

Unpopular decisions, led to

A leadership contest, and she

Left No 10 with tears in her eyes,

And a knife in her back. But this

So called 'Iron Lady', left a lasting

Impression of austerity, and

Contempt for the lower classes.

Murmuration

At dusk, thousands

Of starlings sweep

Back and forth, trying

To avoid predators,

Before going to roost.

No Going Back

Discovering I'd been

Adopted, after sixty years,

I shrugged my shoulders,

And carried on regardless.

Blue Heaven

When walking through

The woods in springtime,

I drown in a sea of

Bluebells; with the sound

Of the blackbird singing.

In The Balance

Experts agree, too many people.

But too many old, and not enough

Young, is going to cause problems.

Miscalculation by governments.

Worlds Apart

Nature

Has all

The answers,

But can

Science

Unlock

Her secrets?

Communion

In the afternoon, I walked

Through the woods, and down

A path to a secluded cove,

Where I walked around the

Headland, before the tide came

In, but as I turned the corner

Everything went silent; and

Above my head, set back on

The hill, a brilliant white

Light between two trees; but

In an instant, it was gone

And the silence was broken.

Somewhat bewildered, I returned

To the beach; but some

Years later, I was reminded

Of the incident, when a medium

Told me 'You've seen God!'

Rise And Fall

At sunrise, a ball
Of liquid gold; at sunset, a
Red balloon deflating.

Future

Half human,
Half machine,
Three – quarters
Robotic; total
Assimilation,
Human replacement.

Ancient And Modern

Since time
Immemorial
Empires built
On the back
Of slavery.

Red Tape

Town and country

Councils, are the

Hub of regulations,

They teach their

Staff to fill in

Forms, and never

Show compassion.

The Power of Love

When true love strikes,

The heart is punctured,

Emotion fills the troubled mind.

But happiness in its purest form

Is the love between two people.

Serial Killer

He is a wolf in
Sheep's clothing, with
The power of life
And death; he takes
Pleasure in stalking
His prey, and watching
His victims suffer, but
Allowed to remain free
Is his licence to
Slaughter; the need
To kill is genetic.

Rush Hour

Rushing
Here and
Rushing
There, no
Time for
Living.

Evolution Gone Mad

Because Darwin
Said we came from
Apes, Adam changed
Into 'Tarzan' and Eve
Become Jane and
Fed him bananas.

Second Coming

Four billion years
Before the sun
Explodes, and a
Thousand trillion
Before the cosmos
Freezes. Time for
Another 'Big Bang',
God willing.

Easy Meat

The internet is the
Devil's playground and
His mark is on every
Page; his favourite game
Is hide – and – seek, and
You never see him coming.

Spontaneous Decision

Is it
Best to
Think
First or
Act first
Before
Thinking?

Endless Night

Dark energy,

Dark matter,

Black hole,

Singularity.

Dark Lord,

Antimatter,

Dark Web,

Black eternity.

Polaroid

The brain is like a

Camera: it absorbs the light, and

Turns it into pictures.

Unity

Forget about ideology.

Governments must swallow

Their pride, and come together

For the greater good, and

Help the world to survive.

Interplanetary

Seven months to

Get there, six

To get back. Only

One survived, the

Rest went mad.

Factors

The most complicated
Equation, is the one
That defines the
Perfect human being.

Loophole

If crime
Doesn't pay,
Why do
Barristers defend
The guilty?

History In the Making

Whatever happened in the
Past, can affect the present, and
Change the future.

Overgrown

Bitterness and resentment
Are deep – rooted; they block
The road to reconciliation.

Foretold

In my early twenties,
I was told by a medium I
Would write a book; I've
Written five already, but
This is the one he meant.

Tolerance

Her husband left her, for
Her best friend, but she swallowed her
Pride, and she kept her son.

Next Generation

An algorithm of being human,

Created by man, transferred

To a robot, and computer

Driven – a hybrid being, but

Given time, will merge into

One, and change evolution.

Out Of Control

Soon, you will

Need a degree,

Just to exist

In this God

Forsaken world.

Kid's Stuff

On hearing the Queen
Had Covid-19, at the
Age of 95, a young girl
Remarked 'We get a week
Off school if she dies!'

Forecast

We call incoming
Storms by Christian
Names, like Dudley,
Eunice, Franklin.
Beware of Beelzebub.

Leader

The most

Dangerous

Man in the

World, is the

Rat in the

Corner, with

His finger

On the button.

The Unexpected

When using

Brute force

Against a

Weaker opponent,

Watch out

For resilience

And solidarity.

High Stakes
(2022)

After WW2, the cold war
Started; it stopped for a
While, but has reappeared.
And around the table are
All the players – democracy –
Communism – dictators and
Terrorists.; and with a toxic
Misc. of suspicion and hate,
They all have a chance at
World domination; one roll
Of the dice could decide
The winner, but who will take
The risk? But when Russia
Invaded Ukraine, the world sat
Up and condemned the action.
A glimmer of hope, on the
Road to a peaceful future?

Crunch Time

The spectre of doom

That plagues mankind

Is his need to kill and

Go to war; but if we

Get it wrong, it's an

Early grave, and only

God will shed a tear.

Sacred Earth

God is not a scientist.

He created science, his DNA

Is rooted in nature.

Invasion
(Ukraine 2022)

For whatever reason, an

Unprovoked attack on

A sovereign country is

An act of war; but if

Intervention could make

Things worse, its better

To wait, and stand united,

Against an aggressor

Who would use the bomb.

A New Direction

A world in crisis,

Needs a brand new

System; no more borders

Between East and West.

A New World Order.

A peaceful place, led

By ordinary people.

Dawn Chorus

At the break of day,

The wonderous sound

Of angels singing; the

Voice of God, through

A blackbird speaking.

Middle Ground

From the sublime

To the ridiculous

With nothing in between,

There must be a

Better way, or is

It just a dream?

Problem Solved

In the beginning, was
God a good teacher, or,
The ultimate dictator? –
'Do as I say, or else!'
But forget about Eden,
And Eve's temptation,
Life and death make the
Perfect equation; the
Key to eternal life.

Protector

Somewhere in the
House of Commons,
Is the ghost of
Oliver Cromwell!
Red – faced and spitting.
Venom; time for a
New model party.

Endgame

Closer to the end

Then the beginning.

But my newfound

Roll is making coffee,

Washing – up, cleaning

Clothes, minding the

Dog, while trying to

Finish this book, and

Playing my didgeridoo.

Age Of Consent

If medically speaking,

The human brain is not

Fully grown until 25,

Who decided 18 is better?

Potential

However limited, our need
To learn, is only matched by
Our thirst for knowledge.

Pitfalls

In a short amount
Of time, the human race
Has come a long way.
Collectively clever, and
Able to adapt, but if
We fall to the foot of the
Mountain, there is no way
Back to the summit.

Our Closet Neighbour

Bonobo monkeys are
The perfect primate.
Regular sex, no class
System, conflict free,
A joyful existence.

Afterlife

With your final breath, your

Body dies; but your soul lives

On in a different world.

The Impossible Dream

I dare to dream

Of a world without

Fear, a peaceful

Place, where greed and

Power have disappeared.

Start To Finish

Behind a wall

Of solid rock,

We climb

The stairs till we

Reach the top,

Where all our

Achievements are

Closely assessed,

And used in a

Passport for the

Journey ahead.

Genius

Theory and practice,

Visionary, or nuts and

Bolts; but put them

Both together, and create

The perfect balance.

Prophecy

Blue is the colour

Of God's own planet.

The perfect environment

To produce mankind –

Full of potential – the

Sky's the limit; but

Power and aggression will

Lead to destruction, and

Return planet Earth

To Mother Nature.

Incompatible

Conform,

Or else.

Conform

Be damned!

Bricklayer

Victorian engineering was

Built to last, stronger than steel

In underground tunnels.

Wisdom In Action

In the end

Solomon was

Right, common

Sense is the

Greatest gift.

Russian Roulette

I'm sick of world

Leaders threatening the

Lives of ordinary

People, in their search

For world domination.

Out – Of – Body

I woke up this morning and
Thought I was dead; I went
Downstairs but remained in bed.

Hybrid

A I means computers.
Humans are organic.
But mix them both
Together, is a robot
With a conscience, or
An alien spitting acid.

Tartan

A textile design with
Checks and stripes, colour
Combinations for different
Clans, worn in battle and
The Highland Games, official
Functions and marching bands.

The Rape of South Wales

From Cardiff to Swansea
In the 19th century, the
Land was ravaged by
Industrialization; stripped
Of its minerals, until the
Market crashed, and left to
Rot, with its heart ripped
Out. But a carpet of green
Now covers the valleys,
Hiding the scars and the
Violation; and a fitting
Tribute to the men of Wales
Is they shared their wealth
With the rest of the world.

Pecking Order

The upper class make the laws,
The middle class make the money,
The lower class do their best,
But its all about the system.

Angels And Demons

If you believe in God
You must believe in Satan.
But if you believe in
Nothing, you're neither good
Or evil, but just an
Observer on the field of battle.

Rest In Peace

First the heart stops, and
Then the brain, as we drift away
To the land of dreams.

Busy Little Bee

We seek it here,
We seek it there,
That elusive drone
Is everywhere; is
It above, or is it
Below, that darn
Elusive probing eye.

Impact

Who will history remember, the
Man devoted to others, or the tyrant
With blood on his hands?

For God's Sake
(The Bottom Line)

In the book of Genesis, God
Punished mankind with certain
Death, for eating forbidden
Fruit; but in the New Testament,
His only son is sacrificed for the
Sins of man, with the promise of
Eternal life. It's all very
Difficult to understand, and yet
Here we are in the 21st century,
A bloody disgraceful, chaotic
Mess; never asking to be born,
But terrified of dying; so why
Are we here? What is the point?
Only God knows all the answers.

Fire and Ice

The cold war in

Europe is about

To get colder, even

Artic if the truth

Be told, as a fire – wall

Is lowered between

East and West, a

Single spark could

Ignite the world.

Rush Hour

He lived his life

In the fast lane,

Not enough time

In the day, until he

Had a heart attack,

But the ambulance

Arrived too late.

Mind – Blowing

Abstract art is hard
To copy if it's 'Lavender Mist'.
By Jackson Pollock.

Rat Poison

While families in their
Houses sleep, the government
Rats begin to speak, making
Laws for us to follow,
Then sitting back to watch
Us suffer; unless we
Escape the elitist trap.

Cybercops

Gone are the days of the
Horse and plough, the
Pitchfork and the tractor,
We plant the seed and
Harvest crops, with machines,
The require no humans.

Constituent Parts

Kindness,
Corruption,
Deception,
Collusion.
Violence,
Compassion,
Depression,
Confusion,
Tolerance,
Aggression,
Jealousy,
Impatience.
Anger,
Desire,
Arrogance,
Suspicion.
All working
Parts of
The human
Condition.

Genesis

Out of the void came

Illumination, the face

Of God in all his glory,

His sacred blood is radiation,

And his body the tree of life.

Eye Of the Beholder

Glass half empty,

Glass half full,

Front door, back

Door, inside out.

Forged original.

Genuine; fake, only

A blind man

Can see the truth.

Crash Course

We came down from

The trees, to live on

The land, and have

Kept on the road to a

Better future, but

Driven by science to the

Edge of the cliff,

We either move forward,

Or take a step back.

Medium
(The Art of Scrying)

In front of a jet –

Black mirror, staring

At his own reflection,

Until another face

Replaced his own, but

Was it angel or demon?

Endeavour

We ride the waves of

An endless ocean, in search of

Our place in history.

Freedom

I don't believe in government.

I don't believe in rules, i

Don't believe in marriage, and

Having lots of children; but

I have a moral compass, and it's

Always pointing North, across

Open fields, and wooded hills,

To the mountain tops beyond.

Stalker

Death is

Always

One step

Behind

The living.

Eternity

The key to

Life is to

Live forever.

Forget about

Death, it's

About the

Here after.

Extermination

They came from all over Europe; the
Jews, the gypsies, the homosexuals.
Squeezed into trucks and transported
By rail, to the infamous camp called
Auschwitz. Once through the gates,
Their fate was decided; immediate
Death or work and starvation.
Hitler's favourites, the SS guards,
Would deliver the 'Final Solution'.
Gas chambers were very effective but
Cremation became a problem, which meant
The rest were shot in the head, and
Buried in enormous pits. Mountains
Of clothing, glasses and shoes, gold
Extracted from victim's teeth, the
Orchestra played, the residents sang, but
Nobody came to save them. And at the end
Of the war, at the Commandant's trial,
He denied any cover – up, and showed no
Remorse, but unless we learn to live in
Peace, ideology will destroy us all.

Omen

The iceberg that

Sank the Titanic,

Is back in the

North Atlantic.

The Indian Ocean.

The South Pacific.

A Moment in Time

Outside the sound

Of heavy traffic; car

Doors slamming, loud

Music playing; dogs

Barking, people chatting.

And in amongst it

All, the sound of a blackbird singing.

I, Parasite

While standing still, the
Rest moved forward; left to live
On the back of others.

Out Of Sight

Monsters don't
Live in cages.
They live next
Door, and move
In higher places.

At Dawn
(WW1)

Waiting in line

For the whistle

To blow; then

Over the top

Into the jaws

Of hell; through

No – man's – land,

With rifle in

Hand, he ran for

His life, but was

Killed in action.

Red Tape

It's hard to

Make things

Simple; but

Easy to make

Them difficult.

Unfair

Did poorly at school, a
Low paid job, one failed marriage,
Won twenty million quid.

Untarnished

Politicians who
Become leaders,
Get others to do
The dirty work,
While appearing
Squeaky – clean.

Monitored

Blues on the right,

Reds on the left,

Yellow in the middle.

But join them together,

And call it coalition.

With no prime minister,

President or general, but

Elected teams with

Workable plans, in rooms

With hidden cameras.

Single – Minded

We are all human

Beings; we all have

Brains; but it's

What we learn from

An early age, that

Makes us individual.

Ourselves To Blame

It's coming, it's coming,
Its already here! The spectre
Of doom is walking the
Earth: the horsemen are riding,
I can hear the hooves as
Nuclear war creeps ever closer.
Pandemic, floods, fire and
Drought, it's all in the book
Of revelation, and with
Armageddon just around the corner,
We must prepare for the worst,
And pray for forgiveness.

Flashbacks

As the sun goes down,
It's all the memories
That come flooding back,
That make a life worthwhile.

Stalwarts

Women are the backbone

Of society, they suffer in

The name of childbirth.

Straight And Narrow

When young, we believe

What we're told, but as

We get older, we question

What's right, and make

Any minor adjustments.

Fireworks

Ten thousand bombs, stacked

Neatly in rows, require one spark,

To ignite the world.

Unpredictable

It's for certain

We are going

To die; it's the

Uncertainty of

Where and how.

Second Chance

Back through the

Mountains, back through

The jungle, back

Through the desert, back

Through the oceans.

Let's start again,

From the very beginning –

Back to basics, with

Hope in abundance.

Imagination

A creative hub, in black

And white; vivid colours; illusion and

Reality rolled into one.

Leap Of Faith

Compared with some, i

Haven't done a lot, one

Of life's underachievers,

Who's just drifted along,

It's too late to change

Into something I'm not,

Or fret about the past and

Opportunities lost, but here

I am, at the edge of the cliff,

Perhaps I should jump,

And hope for the best.

Iron Curtain 2

An angry bear invaded
His neighbour, set Europe on fire,
Showed the west whose boss.

Diplomacy

Promises, promises, all
Hot air, unwilling to talk,
Unwilling to share, with
Time and patience running
Out, a willingness to try,
Is the key to success.

For Better or Worse

On the final day, we
Must walk away, and
Face the truth of what
We've achieved, and
Accept the verdict,
Come what may, and
Go our separate ways.

Beautiful Curse

Free – will, is the

Freedom to choose,

Between reaching the

Top or falling down,

But its better

Then being oppressed.

Revolution

A fundamental mistake,

To create machines cleverer than us,

The price is self – destruction.

Spread Your Wings

Umbilical cord,

Apron strings,

School and college,

Going steady.

Marriage vows,

Successful job,

Having children,

Mortgage repayments.

Playing sport,

Social ladder,

Retirement pensions,

Funeral plans.

But before it's

Too late, release

The chains, and

Go in search

Of Shanghai – la.

Soundscape

From the initial bang,
To the present day,
Acoustics, vibrations,
Musical notes; the
Harmonic code keeps
The cosmos spinning.
God with earphones
In all his glory.

Conflict

I sit on the
Fence between
Good and evil,
Neither one nor
The other, but
Both together.
With free will
To choose, or
Remain agnostic.

Humanoid

We are but

Cogs in a huge

Machine, soon

To be replaced

By microchips.

Law – Abiding

Laws are conceived.

By man, except the

Ten Commandments; used.

And amended through

Social change, and

Scientific advancement.

Elizabeth R
(1926 – 2022)

The longest serving
British Monarch, seventy
Years as Head of State,
Steadfast, devout,
She did her duty,
The ultimate constant
Defender of the faith.

Royalty

A ruby rose, with
Emerald leaves, protected
By thorns, surrounded
By weeds and nettles.

Once And for All

The only cure for
Rising tension between
The East and West,
Is to do what they did
To Japan in 1945.

Obsession
(War Against Ukraine 2022)

Invade,
Advance,
Retreat,
Recruit.
Attack.
NEVER
Give in.
Achieve
Your goal
At any cost.
The end
Result is
All that
Matters.

Life After Death

What happens, when

Our eyelids close for

The final time? Look

No further than sea

And sand, and the sound

Of good vibrations.

One Step Behind

Keep walking straight

Towards the light, and

Never look back at

The faceless being, who

Wants to take your life.

Knife – Edge
(2022)

If living on the edge is your
Thing, now is the perfect time; the
Constant threat of nuclear war,
Overpopulation, climate change,
The lack of food and water; and
All we can do is sit and watch,
While others decide our future.

Enough Is Enough

It's all too much,
The push and shove,
The rushing about,
The couldn't care
Less, life in the fast
Lane is no life at
All, no time to breathe,
Until you are dead.

Uncharted

Trying to navigate

The rationale, is like sailing the

Oceans without a compass.

Pied Piper

It's all so easy,

Just go on – line, use

Your app and mobile

Phone; on – line banking,

On – line shopping, on –

Line chatting, on – line

Scamming; whatever you

Want it's all on – line,

Just tap your keyboard

And follow – the – leader.

10/10/53

If it takes a bang

On the head, to increase

Your senses, I thank

The driver who ran

Me over, aged five.

Seer

Fear not, according

To Nostradamus, mankind

Will still be here

In 7074, so stop worrying,

Sit – back and relax.

Embolism

Inside the body,

It follows the stream, searching for

Places to block the flow.

Split Decision

When making choices, instinct
Tells us to use our gut, instead
Of rational thinking.

Elixir of Life

Modern day
Drugs help
The old live
Longer, and
The young
From dying.

Clinical

No more air raids,
Trench warfare,
Or hand – to hand
Fighting; because
Nuclear war is
Quick and painless,
Except for those
In Bunkers.

Tradition

Opening the window
After people have
Died, is still observed,
By those who believe
The soul has wings.

Independence Day

A robotic arm
With AI intelligence,
Lost its temper
When told it had
Made a mistake.

Age Concern

It creeps up.
And before you
Know it you're
Slowing down,
Taking tablets,
Receding inwards.
But all is not
Lost, if you open
The windows, and
Keep moving on.

Knowledge

All the problems now
Facing mankind, come from the
Lack of education.

Heaven and Hell

Almighty, perfect,
Full of love; a
Forgiving God; until
You cross the line,
Where wrath and
Retribution reveals
His darker side.

Bruise

Blood thinning
Tablets prevent
Clots forming
But encourage
Internal bleeding.

Journey

Life and death

Are intertwined.

And when it comes

To health, we must

Hope for the best.

But weather short

Or long, we must

Accept our fate,

And believe our

Lives have purpose.

Side Effects

Some are common,

Others are rare,

But weather its

Drugs, or human

Behaviour, we have

To adapt, and

Adjust psychologically.

Mechanics

Without the heart, the

Brain can't function.

Without the brain, the

Heart stops beating.

But joined together, they

Keep the body working.

Trust

My dog George

Has a habit

Of staring, but

There is no malice,

Jealousy or hate,

Only love and

Affection for the

Man, who feeds him.

Forever Young

Growing old is

Natural, staying

Young is not,

But keeping young

While growing

Old, is all

We really want.

The Unknown

Nobody asks to be

Born; but here we

Are, for better or

Worse, and for whatever

Reason: until we face

The final act, when

Death steps in, and

Unlocks the door.

Ecocide

On the incoming tide

Came a man – made monster.

Full of revenge, He devoured

The coast, and reduced

The land to desert.

Sitting Target

In times of war,

The armies fight,

The civilians suffer.

Race Related

Not in monochrome,

Or shades of colour,

But through rose –

Coloured glasses, we

All look the same.

Conviction

Religious freedom
Within the law is
Acceptable; but
Whichever God you
Choose to follow,
Stay true to
What you believe.

Eye For an Eye

I couldn't become
A policeman, a
Barrister, or judge,
Because I believe
In justice, which has
All but disappeared.

Sugar and Spice

Children are like a
Ball and chain; sugar – coated with
A stubborn nature.

Brought To Book

Politicians who waste
Our money, and those
Who take backhanders,
Should go to jail, and
Stripped of any honours.

Food For Thought

In the animal kingdom,

Hunger can prove fatal.

But in our society,

Poverty and hardship go

Hand – in hand, and the

Only difference between

Them and us, is they

Kill to survive, while

We depend on money.

National Heroes Society

Open – heart surgery

Aged eleven; open –

Heart surgery aged

Seventy-five; I've

Certainly, had my monies

Worth, and they

Keep on saving lives.

In a Nutshell

With all things
Considered, it's
Family that matters
At the end of the day.

Hypocrisy

I've never heard of league
Tables for politicians; but
If they existed, most would
Fail miserably; too much
Talking, not enough action.

Bridge

Nobody knows why
We have to die,
Except the creator,
On the other side
Of the great divide.

First Contact

Look into the

Eyes of nature,

And see the

Face of God!

Top of the Bill
(For Steven Billing, 31.1.2023)

My cardiac surgeon is one

Of the best, when it comes

To valve replacement; his

Surgical team behind closed

Doors perform their act

With skill and precision;

And at the end of a gruelling

Performance, they take a bow

The surgeons, the anaesthetist,

The technicians and nurses;

And with another life saved,

The curtain comes down, to

The sound of a loud applause.

Break Out

Democracy, for so long the leader, is now
Receding towards autocracy; and as
The world becomes our prison, we the
Inmates must make our bid for freedom.

Antidote

The pain of being in
Hospital, is offset by the care,
The friendship, the compassion.

Ordeal

Every experience
To face mankind
Was already here
Before we arrived.
Custom – made for
Each individual,
The journey we take
Is preordained.

Therapy

Finding things that
Make us happy,
Removes the threat
Of negativity.

Survivor

Not as lucky as some,
But more luckier than
Others; but when the
Chips are down, we must
Come up trumps, and
Carry on regardless.

Palm Sunday

On the back of a
Humble donkey; the cross remains, as
His memory Fades.

Sacrifice

Crucifixion is a
Cruel way to die;
Lots of pain and
Suffering, all for
The sins of man.

Defiance

By hook or by crook
We will make you change.
By hook or by crook
I will live my life,
And in my own time.

Faith Rewarded

When our time is up,
Do we go through the
Door in disbelief, or
Put our trust in God?

Out of control

The internet is a lethal
Weapon, in the hands of adults
Who act like children.

Unrestrained

Everyone is capable of
Doing anything, if they
Believe it's possible.

Attitude

If your lucky,
What you put
In is what you
Get out; but if
You don't bother,
Expect nothing back,
Or regret your
Lack of interest.

Eternal

Time is relentless,

Life is enduring,

Death is the end;

Or a new beginning.

Milestone

Tempted by

An older woman;

Rejected after

Twenty years;

Experience is the

Spice of life,

On the long and

Winding road.

Private Retreat

From the horror

Of fighting on

The Western Front,

To the local towns

For sex and drink.

Hereafter

Hitler was a monster;

And even tho he lost the

War, his actions created

The superpowers, and

Broke the British Empire.

People Power

Barring all out

War, peaceful protest

Is the only way, to

Break the status Quo.

DemiGod

With the power of speech

He brainwashed his people;

An Aryan messiah,

Therefore invincible; until

The Russians came and

Destroyed Berlin, and all

Hopes of world domination.

On Balance

Whether by chance,

Good luck or fate,

Being alive is

Better than Dead.

Black Hole

After the Sun has

Gone, only hope can

Save the world, from

The evil pouring in.

Quick Fix

Is an addiction to drugs,
The easy way out of a
Turbulent life? Who knows,
Unless you try it first.

Short- Sighted

The principle of an eye for an
Eye, depends where you live, and
Which religion you follow; but
The basic idea is a life for a life,
And not fifteen years in prison.

Closure

The Lord is.

My shepherd,

I shall not

Want. He leads.

Me beside

Quiet waters,

And I will

Fear no evil.

Amen.

At the point of death reality ends,
The world of spirit begins.

www.ingramcontent.com/pod-product-compliance
Lightning Source LLC
Chambersburg PA
CBHW050151130526
44591CB00033B/1250